Series 63
Uniform Securities Agent State Law Exam

Student Notebook
2nd Edition

KAPLAN FINANCIAL

SERIES 63 UNIFORM SECURITIES AGENT STATE LAW EXAM, 2ND EDITION ©2007 DF Institute, Inc. All rights reserved.

Published by DF Institute, Inc.

Printed in the United States of America.

ISBN: 1-4277-5805-0

PPN: 3663-1523

07	08	10	9	8	7	6	5	4	3	2	1
J	F	**M**	A	M	J	J	A	S	O	N	D

Kaplan Financial
Securities Courses, Insurance and CPE Continuing Education Request Form

Name _____

Please print your name as you wish it to appear on your certificate

Social Security Number _____ Birth date _____

 # must be provided _required by Indiana_

State License Number (must be provided for insurance CE) _____ / _____

License No. _State_

Address to mail certificate: _____

_____

_CPAs (except in New York) receive credit for most securities prelicensing classes. CFP® certificants must pass the NASD exam and do not require certificates from Kaplan Financial. CPAs receive credit for self-study and computer-based training (except in Florida, Illinois, Montana, Nebraska, and Oregon). If you are a CPA and want CPE credits (except in Florida, Illinois, Montana, Nebraska, and Oregon), check here _____._

FOR CLASSROOM ATTENDANCE:

Which securities class did you attend? _____ When? _____

student must attend every session

Who was your instructor? _____

FOR SELF-STUDY:

If CE credits are approved, mail or fax this form with a copy of test results **AND** a copy of Kaplan Financial invoice to

KAPLAN FINANCIAL
Attn: Securities CE Credits
30 South Wacker Drive
Chicago, IL 60606-7481
Fax: (312) 577-2453 for credit card orders

$15 for first certificate, plus state fees, where applicable. Additional certificates for the same securities course are $10 each. Any additional certificates requested for a different securities course are $15 each. Make checks payable to Kaplan Financial.

Add state fees	CT	MI	NC	NH	OH	PA	WV
per course	$5.00					$5.00	
per credit hour		$1.00	$1.00	$2.00	$1.00		$1.75

☐ Check or money order made payable to Kaplan Financial enclosed

☐ American Express ☐ Discover ☐ Mastercard ☐ Visa

_____ / _____

Card Number Expiration Date

_____ / _____

Authorized Signature Date

Contents

Thank you for choosing Kaplan Financial for your Series 63 exam preparation. This course covers the wide range of topics that the North American Securities Administrators Association (NASAA) has outlined as essential to the Uniform Securities Agent.

This notebook will save you time by covering the main points presented in class and serving as a reference when you review for the exam. Extra space is provided for your notes.

We recommend that you complete all practice questions in this notebook as well as those in the *Series 63 License Exam Manual* before you take the Series 63 exam. You should then take the exam within one week of taking the class.

As always, Kaplan Financial strives to provide you with the most current test preparation information. If you have any questions about this or any other Kaplan Financial study material, please call Kaplan Financial's AnswerPhone at:

1-800-621-9621, ext. 3598

between 8:00 am and 6:00 pm CT, Monday through Friday. AnswerPhone's staff of content experts will answer your questions and clarify the material as needed. Also, be sure to visit Kaplan Financial's Website at **www.kaplanfinancial.com** for the latest industry updates and information on Kaplan Financial study materials.

This course may qualify for CE credit in your state.

The Series 63 Exam consists of 65 multiple-choice questions covering the topics listed below. Applicants are allowed 75 minutes to complete the test. Candidates must attain a score of 70% to pass. Credit will be given for correct answers only. Of the 65 questions on the exam, only 60 will count toward the final score. The remaining 5 questions are being tested for possible inclusion in future exams. These questions may appear anywhere in the exam and are not identified.

SERIES 63 EXAM BREAKDOWN		
Test Topic	**Percentage of Exam**	**No. of Questions**
Registration of Persons	30%	18
Securities	25%	15
Unethical Business Practices	35%	21
Administrative Provisions of the Uniform Securities Act	10%	6
Total	100%	60

Marie Sychowski
Momskie@qwest.net

John Ibis
800.621.9621 X4469

65 questions
75 minutes
70% pass, mid to upper 80% M practice exams

Unit 1
Registration of Persons

 *People*

I. ORIGINS OF THE UNIFORM SECURITIES ACT (USA)

A. PURPOSE

To unify state laws and protect investors

B. USA AS MODEL LEGISLATION

1. First drafted in the mid-1950s

2. Template or guide that each state uses in drafting state securities laws

3. The Series 63 tests on the template, not individual state's versions

II. TERMS

A. ADMINISTRATOR — *State person @ SEC level*

B. PERSONS

1. Any legal being, including an individual, corporation, partnership, association, joint-stock company, unincorporated organization, government, or political subdivision of a government

2. *Person* does not include minor children, individuals declared mentally incompetent, and deceased individuals

3. Substitute term *entity* or *individual* when term *person* is used

C. BROKER/DEALER — *Transactions* *legal entity*
Legal entity *buying securities for others*

1. Any person, not an agent, that is in the business of effecting transactions in securities for accounts of others or its own account

2. Broker/dealer does not include

$ whenever a location on client in state — must register

   a. Agent — *state word Registered Agent*

   b. Issuer

   c. Holding Co.

    c. Bank or trust company

    d. Person with no office in state who effects transactions in state exclusively with or through

        1.) Banks, savings institutions, or trust companies

        2.) Insurance companies

        3.) Investment companies registered under the 1940 Act

        4.) Pension or profit-sharing trusts

        5.) Other broker/dealers

        6.) Existing customers whose residence is not in the state

3. Broker/dealer financial requirements

    a. Administrator may establish minimum capital requirement not to exceed that required under SEC Act of 1934

    b. Administrator may require surety bonds if broker/dealer has custody/discretion

        protect customer if Theft

        1.) Amount of bonds not to exceed the requirements under SEC Act of 1934

        2.) Cash or securities in lieu of bond

D. AGENT

1. An individual representing a broker/dealer or an issuer in attempting to or effecting sales of securities

2. Those meeting the definition must register as agents in the state

3. The term *agent* does not include

    a. An individual who represents the issuer, if no compensation is paid directly or indirectly for soliciting any person in the state, in effecting transactions

        1.) In exempt securities

        2.) In exempt transactions

        3.) With existing employees, partners, officers, or directors of the issuer or any subsidiary

    b. Partners, officers, or directors of broker/dealers who do not effect sales

    c. Clerical and administrative staff of broker/dealers with no sales function

    d. Persons with no place of business in state who sell to existing customers not residents of state

4. Dual registration—if under common control or authorized by the Administrator

owned by same parent co.

5. Commission sharing—if under common control

6. Client moves to another state—agent has 30 days to register

1. According to the USA, which of the following is NOT considered a person?

   A. The custodian of a custodial account where the beneficial owner is a minor
   B. An individual who has not reached the age of majority in the state where he resides
   C. XYZ Corporation, which has just completed its IPO
   D. The city of Pasadena, California

2. Which of the following entities is responsible for the administration of the USA in a state?

   A. State judiciary system
   B. Executive department
   C. The Administrator
   D. Securities and Exchange Commission

3. Under the USA, which of the following would be considered a person?

   I. An unincorporated investment club
   II. An individual who buys and sells securities only for his own account
   III. Associations and partnerships whether or not they issue certificates
   IV. The US government

   A. I only
   B. I, II and III
   C. II and III
   D. I, II, III and IV

4. An agent under the USA is any person who

   I. represents an issuer in nonexempt securities
   II. is a registered broker/dealer who deals in registered securities
   III. sells nonexempt securities as a representative of a registered broker/dealer
   IV. has no place of business in state and sells securities to an existing client who is not a resident of the state

   A. I and II
   B. I and III
   C. II and III
   D. II and IV

5. Which of the following entities is NOT an agent as defined in the USA?

   I. A broker/dealer acting on behalf of a properly registered issuer
   II. An individual who represents US government securities in exempt transactions without any direct or indirect compensation
   III. An individual who sells exempt securities in an exempt transaction for nominal compensation
   IV. An individual who represents an issuer in a nonexempt transaction

   A. I and II
   B. I and III
   C. II and III
   D. II and IV

II.   TERMS (Continued)

E.   NATIONAL SECURITIES MARKETS IMPROVEMENT ACT OF 1996 (NSMIA)

1. Purpose—enacted to eliminate conflicts between federal and state securities laws

2. Covers—federal covered securities and federal covered investment advisers

3. Result—states cannot require registration of securities, transactions or investment advisers covered by or excluded by federal legislation

F.   INVESTMENT ADVISER — *compensation*

1. Defined as "any person who for compensation engages in the business of advising others as to the value of securities or, as part of a regular business, issues analyses or reports concerning securities"

Financial planners – may not always be a B/D charging for advice

2. Also includes financial planners and other persons who provide advice

Financial Planners
Pension Consultants
Sports Agents

G.   INVESTMENT ADVISER DOES NOT INCLUDE

1. Investment adviser representative — ~~Financial planner~~
~~Charged for fee advice~~

2. Bank, savings institution, or trust company

3. Lawyer, Accountant, Teacher, or Engineer with advisory services incidental to the practice

4. Broker/dealer or its agents with incidental advisory services with no special compensation

5. Publisher of a newspaper, column, newsletter, or financial publication of general circulation, that does not render advice on specific investment situation of each client

6. A person who has no place of business in the state and only gives advice to

     a. Other investment advisers

     b. Broker/dealers

c. Financial institutions (banks, insurance companies, and investment companies)

d. Maximum of 5 persons (other than above) during a 12-month period—de minimis exemption

7. Any person who is a federal covered adviser

Wrap Fees—flat fee, must be a I/A

H. FEDERAL COVERED ADVISER

1. Those advisers registered under the Investment Advisers Act of 1940

2. Advisers with $30 million or more in assets under management must register with the SEC as federal covered advisers and as such are covered by federal law

3. Advisers with at least $25 million but less than $30 million in assets under management can register with either the SEC or the state

4. Advisers with less than $25 million under management must register with the state

a. Advisers to registered investment companies are federal covered regardless of the size of the investment company

b. Pension consultants with at least $50 million in assets

c. Covered also means covered by exclusion from the definition

Adviser managing . . .

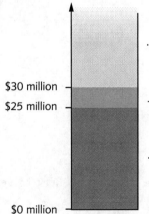

. . . $30 million or more—**SEC** registration

$30 million —

$25 million —

. . . at least $25 million but less than $30 million—**SEC** or **state** registration

. . . less than $25 million—**state** registration

$0 million —

I. INVESTMENT ADVISER REPRESENTATIVE

1. Any partner, officer, or other individual employed by or associated with an investment adviser and

  a. Always an individual

  b. Required to be registered under USA

  c. Makes recommendations or renders advice regarding securities

  d. Manages accounts or portfolios

  e. Determines recommendations

  f. Solicits or sells investment advisory services

  g. Supervises employees who perform any of the above

2. Investment adviser representative must be registered in the state whether associated with a state-registered adviser or with a federal covered adviser

J. ISSUER

1. Issues or proposes to issue any security

  a. Can be corporation, or federal or state government

  b. Foreign government

  c. Partnership

  d. Nonprofit

  e. Cooperative

2. Issuer or primary transaction—for benefit of the issuer

  a. First time an issuer distributes securities to public; issuer receives money

  b. Any other time the issuer receives the proceeds of the sale

3. Nonissuer transaction

  a. Not directly or indirectly for the benefit of the issuer

  b. Secondary market transactions

III.   GENERAL REGISTRATION PROCEDURES FOR SECURITIES PROFESSIONALS

A. <u>SUBMIT APPLICATION</u>

1. Effective at noon of 30th day after filing is completed   *– people B/D, IAR, IA, A*

2. Renews each December 31   *– people*

3. Successor investment advisory firm fees good until renewal date

B. PROVIDE CONSENT TO SERVICE OF PROCESS

1. With initial filing only—permanent document

2. All registrants: issuers, broker/dealers, investment advisers, agents, and investment adviser representatives

C. PAY FILING FEES

D. PRESENT FINANCIAL REPORTS AND RECORDKEEPING REPORTS AS REQUIRED

1. Broker/dealers and investment advisers only

2. Broker/dealer records—3 years

3. Investment advisers—5 years

E. FINANCIAL REQUIREMENTS

1. Broker/dealer: may be required

2. Agent/investment adviser representative: none

3. Investment adviser: may be required

F. POST SURETY BONDS OR DEPOSIT CASH OR SECURITIES

1. Agent or investment adviser representative—if exercising discretion

2. Broker/dealer—if discretion or custody over customer funds and securities, (unless sufficient net capital)

3. Investment adviser—if discretion or custody over customer funds and securities, (unless sufficient net worth)

4. Bonding against employee embezzlement and theft

G. PASS EXAM, WRITTEN AND/OR ORAL

1. Broker/dealer

2. Agent

3. Investment adviser

4. Investment adviser representative

H. WITHDRAWAL OF REGISTRATION

1. Voluntary withdrawal effective on 30th day

2. Agent termination requires notice to Administrator by agent and broker/dealer

3. Investment adviser representative termination requires notice to Administrator by investment adviser only if a state-covered investment adviser

4. Investment adviser representative termination requires notice to Administrator by investment adviser representative only if with a federal covered investment adviser

if fed covered the IAR notifies

Form ADV form Investment Advisor reg on

1. Which of the following is defined as an investment adviser under the Uniform Securities Act?
   I. Investment adviser representative of an advisory firm who makes securities recommendations on a regular basis for compensation
   II. Temporary employee hired to assist in administrative responsibilities of an advisory firm
   III. Any person who is a federal covered investment adviser
   IV. A person who, on a regular basis for compensation, offers specific investment advice to clients as to the value of securities
   A. I and IV
   B. II and III
   C. II and IV
   D. IV only

2. Which of the following is engaging in activities that define a broker/dealer for purposes of state regulation?
   A. An individual, not an agent, with no office in the state who sells government securities to financial institutions in the state
   B. A person, not an agent, with no office in the state who conducts business in securities with trust companies located in the state
   C. A person, not an agent, with an office in the state who sells securities to nonresidents of the state
   D. A person, not an agent, with no office in the state who sells securities to nonresidents of the state

3. According to the USA, which of the following statements is TRUE?
   A. If an agent is hired away from his broker/dealer by another broker/dealer, only the new broker/dealer must notify the Administrator.
   B. If an investment adviser representative is hired away from a federal covered investment adviser by another federal covered adviser, both advisers and the representative must notify the Administrator.
   C. Only the employing adviser, not the investment adviser representative, must register in the state.
   D. An investment adviser with no place of business in the state who conducts business exclusively with insurance companies located in the state need not register in the state.

4. An investment adviser need not register in a state if it has
   A. a place of business in the state and only advises employee benefit plans with less than $1 million
   B. no place of business, does not direct business communications in the state, and advises more than 5 high-net-worth individuals located in the state
   C. a place of business in the state and advises fewer than 5 banks
   D. no place of business in the state and advises only 3 registered investment companies located in the state

5. Which of the following statements are TRUE?

   I. A federal covered adviser is defined as one who sells federal covered securities.

  II. Federal covered advisers are those advisers with federally imposed exemptions from state registration as investment advisers.

 III. A federal covered security is exempt from registration with the SEC.

 IV. Federal covered securities include those issued by investment companies registered under the Investment Company Act of 1940.

  A. I and II

  B. I and III

  C. II and IV

  D. III and IV

I. TERMS

A. SECURITY

Under securities law, a security is defined as an investment of money in a common enterprise with the expectation of profits from the managerial efforts of a third party (the Howey Decision)

1. Under USA, securities include

   a. Stock

   b. Treasury stock

   c. Bond

   d. Note

   e. Debenture

   f. Evidence of indebtedness (promissory note)

   g. Investment contract

   h. Certificate of interest in a profit-sharing or partnership agreement

   i. Certificate of deposit of a security (ADR)

   j. Collateral trust certificate

   k. Preorganization certificate or subscription

   l. Voting trust certificate

   m. Warrant, right, or option for a security

   n. Variable annuity or variable life insurance policy

   o. Certificate of interest or participation in an oil, gas, or mining title

   p. Any interest or instrument commonly known as a security

> **1.)** Oil and gas drilling programs
>
> **2.)** Real estate condominium cooperatives with rental pool arrangement
>
> **3.)** Farm lands or animals (racehorse)

q. Commodity option contracts   *Yes*

r. Whiskey warehouse receipts

s. Multilevel distributorship arrangements

t. Merchandising marketing programs

u. Single stock futures   *CMO, REITS*

v. Negotiable (jumbo) bank certificate of deposit

2. Under USA, security does not include

a. Fixed insurance or annuity contracts

b. Retirement plans (IRA or Keogh) - *planned Document*

c. Collectibles

d. Commodities and commodity futures   *NO*

e. Condominiums used as personal residence

f. Currency

g. Nonnegotiable bank CD

h. Trade confirmation

3. It is much easier to remember the 8 items that are not securities than all of the items that are securities

II.   GENERAL REGISTRATION PROCEDURES UNDER THE USA

A.   FILE REGISTRATION STATEMENT

1. Filing fees

2. Ongoing financial reporting—not more than quarterly

3. Escrow—may be required if security was issued

    a. Within last 3 years

    b. At a price substantially different from offering price

    c. For a consideration other than cash

4. Provide a consent to service of process

B. EFFECTIVE PERIOD OF REGISTRATION

III. METHODS OF SECURITY REGISTRATION — *Apper work to Fed or State*

A. NOTICE FILING — *Investment Companies / Notice to state we are coming in - reg u. the Fed*

1. Primarily used with investment companies registered under the Investment Company Act of 1940

2. Administrator may require fees — *State can collect fees.*

B. COORDINATION — *IPO, multistate*

1. Securities eligible—new shares

2. Required documentation

    a. Three copies of latest prospectus

    b. Copies of articles of incorporation, underwriter agreements, a specimen of security

    c. Any amendments to prospectus filed with SEC

3. Effective date — *concurrent Fed & State*

    a. Simultaneously with federal registration   *Administrator may issue a stop order*

    b. No stop order or proceeding is pending

If Fed says yes the state may say No

    c. Registration on file for minimum time period specified by Administrator

    d. Statement of maximum and minimum proposed offering prices and maximum underwriting compensation on file for 2 full business days

C. QUALIFICATION — *Intrastate* — *A single State*
Fed steps aside for state

1. Relevant information on issuer as determined by Administrator

2. Used for intrastate offerings

3. Any security eligible

4. Application must contain

    a. Issuer's name, address, and form of organization

    b. General character and nature of issuer's business

    c. Description of issuer's physical properties and equipment

    d. Statement of condition of industry or business in which issuer intends to engage

    e. Type and amount of securities offered, proposed offering price, and aggregate selling and underwriting discounts

    f. Estimated proceeds and purpose for use

    g. Copies of prospectus, pamphlet, circular, form letter, advertisement, or other sales literature intended to be used with offering

    h. Any additional information Administrator requires

5. Effective date—Administrator determines

D. PROVISIONS APPLICABLE TO ALL STATE REGISTRATION METHODS

1. Filing fees prorated if filing is withdrawn

2. Registration statement filed by issuer, any other person on whose behalf offering is made, or a registered broker/dealer

3. Specify

    a. Amount of securities offered in the state

not in total

    b. Any adverse order or judgment by a regulatory authority or the SEC

4. Administrator may require, as a condition of registration by qualification or coordination, that securities be sold on a specified form of subscription to be filed with Administrator

5. Issuer may reference previously filed documents if they are current and accurate and within 5 years for a similar security

6. Administrator has power to permit omission of any item of information from registration documentation

1. Which of the following is NOT a security?

   A. An annuity contract that systematically pays a fixed dollar amount to the annuitant

   B. An annuity contract that pays income that attempts to keep pace with inflation

   C. A lower than investment grade bond issued by a plastics company located in another state

   D. Common stock issued by a local manufacturing company

2. Provisions generally applicable to the registration of securities under the Uniform Securities Act would include all of the following EXCEPT

   A. paying a filing fee

   B. filing a consent to service of process

   C. listing all states in which the issue is being registered and the amount of securities being sold in each of them

   D. the proposed use of the proceeds of the issue

3. All of the following must be specified in the state registration statement of a security EXCEPT

   A. a stop order from another state that affects the offering of the security within that state

   B. the total amount of the security that will be offered in other states

   C. the amount of securities to be offered in the state

   D. the expected use of the projected proceeds of the offering

4. Which of the following is an issuer of securities?

   I. A corporation that proposes to issue securities but has not as yet

   II. A broker/dealer who trades for the accounts of others

   III. A new company that offers shares to the public

   IV. A company offering shares in a primary transaction not exempt from registration

   A. I only

   B. I, III and IV

   C. III and IV

   D. I, II, III and IV

5. Which of the following securities would have to be registered by qualification under the Uniform Securities Act?

   I. ABC, Inc., formed 2 years ago and filed with the SEC, previously made an offering of its stock in several other states and now wishes to make a new offering of stock in this state.

   II. XYZ, Inc., plans to make an offering of its stock in only 1 state and so will not file a federal registration statement.

   III. AAA, Inc., is 1 year old, and an initial offering of its stock will be offered in several states at once.

   A. I and II

   B. I and III

   C. II only

   D. I, II and III

Fed Counsel – IBM No Notice
No Notice
Investment Co
Mutual Fund must give not

IV. EXEMPT SECURITIES UNDER THE USA

A. SHORT-TERM NOTES/DEBT OBLIGATIONS

1. Maturity—270 days or less

2. Minimum $50,000 denomination and 3 highest ratings

   a. Commercial paper

   b. Bankers' acceptances

B. SECURITIES ISSUED BY EXEMPT ISSUERS

At state level

State only
1) Federal Political Subdivisions

2) Foreign National Gov.

3) Public Utility

4) Common Carrier

5) Insurance Co

Mexico = no reg
Mexico City = reg

1. US government and agencies

2. Municipalities

3. Canadian government (federal and political subdivisions but not corporations)
State only

4. Issued or guaranteed by foreign national governments with diplomatic relations, (but not their municipalities)
State only

5. Financial institution securities

   a. National and state banks, savings institution, or trust company

   b. Federal savings and loan associations

   c. State chartered savings and loan authorized to do business in this state

   d. Federal credit union or any other credit union supervised under the laws of this state

6. Insurance companies

Fed Res b/c not at State level

   a. Stock and bonds issued by insurance companies authorized to do business in this state

   b. Not variable contracts

7. Public utility companies and common carriers—regulated by state or federal agency
State only

8. Charitable, religious, and nonprofit organizations
State

9. Investment contracts issued in connection with any employee benefit plan
State

C. SECURITIES OF NONEXEMPT ISSUERS

1. National Securities Markets Improvement Act of 1996 (NSMIA)

2. Federally imposed exemption from state securities registration *because of who*

a. Securities listed or authorized for listing on recognized exchanges or quoted on Nasdaq National Market (NNM) securities (Effective July 1, 2006—Global and Global Select)

b. Investment companies registered under the Investment Company Act
must use notice filing

c. Securities exempted under the Securities Act of 1933 — *because who the issuer is*

Exemptions given to the "what"

1.) Governments and agencies

2.) Municipals, (but not in state of issuance)

3.) Nonprofit organizations

Jumbo CD's
Investment Contracts

Fed Exempt then no State reg Needed —
Exempt on both level

1) US Gov

2) Charitible, Religous, Nonprofit's

3) Municipal

4) Banks, Savings, & Loans

Non-Exempt = Corporate

1. Which of the following phrases describe federal covered securities?

   I. A security required to be registered under USA
   II. A security that is registered under the Investment Company Act of 1940
   III. A security of a bank regulated by the US Federal Reserve Board
   IV. A security that the US government issued

   A. I only
   B. II and III
   C. II and IV
   D. II, III and IV

2. All of the following are exempt from state registration EXCEPT

   A. bank stocks
   B. public utility stocks
   C. bonds issued by the German government
   D. stock issued by a local manufacturer

3. Which of the following best describes the effect of the NSMIA on securities regulation?

   A. Established the need for dual registration of securities
   B. Increased the power of state securities Administrators over registration of securities
   C. Provided for the registration of intrastate securities
   D. Preempts state registration of covered securities

4. Which of the following securities are exempt from the registration requirements of the Uniform Securities Act?

   I. An investment contract issued in connection with an employee pension plan
   II. Securities issued by St. Paul's Catholic Church in Tempe, Arizona
   III. Securities issued by a public utility
   IV. Securities issued by the Canadian government

   A. I, II and III
   B. I and III
   C. II and IV
   D. I, II, III and IV

5. Which of the following are included in the definition of federal covered security?

   I. Common stock of ABC Corporation, domiciled in Delaware, listed on the NYSE, and sold to a resident of Delaware
   II. Common stock of ABC Corporation domiciled in Delaware, listed on the NYSE, and sold to a resident of Maryland
   III. City of Portland, Maine GO Bond sold to a resident of Augusta, Maine
   IV. City of Portland, Maine GO Bond sold to a resident of Augusta, Georgia

   A. I and II
   B. I, II and IV
   C. II, III and IV
   D. I, II, III and IV

V.   EXEMPT TRANSACTIONS IN NONEXEMPT SECURITIES

A.   TRADED THROUGH EXEMPT TRANSACTIONS

1. Preorganization certificates

    a. Before incorporation (promise of seed money)

    b. Maximum of 10 subscribers and no funds paid in

2. Private placements — *Selling to institutions*
— mom & pops

    a. Restricted to 10 offers in any 12 consecutive months other than to institutional clients

    b. No immediate resale except for institutions *mom & pop / institutions can flip it*

    c. No compensation paid on sales to noninstitutional buyers *— sold to mom & pop*

    d. May not be advertised

Circumstances have exempted

3. Issuer transactions—between issuer and underwriters (going public)

4. With financial institutions (sophisticated/professional investor)

    a. Investment companies

    b. Insurance companies

    c. Banks and trust companies

    d. Employee benefit plans with over $1 million in assets

        1.) Pension or profit-sharing trusts

    e. Broker/dealers

    f. Investment advisers

5. Nonissuer transactions (secondary transactions)

    a. Unsolicited nonissuer transactions effected through broker/dealer

        1.) Administrator may request proof

    b. Isolated nonissuer transactions

        1.) Generally transactions between individual investors on a private basis

6. Fiduciary transactions

    a. Those by an executor, administrator, trustee, sheriff, and so forth *, custodian*

7. Liquidation of securities pledged as collateral for a loan

8. Offers to existing employees and shareholders of the issuer

    a. No commissions are paid

    b. Example: Preemptive rights offering

The who
The what
T

1. All of the following are exempt transactions EXCEPT
    I. an administrator sells securities to liquidate an estate
    II. a client, upon his own initiative, requests a transaction in a security that is not registered in the state
    III. a fiduciary pledges securities to secure a loan for a client
    IV. a certified financial planner sells Nasdaq securities to numerous high-net-worth individual clients

    A. I and II
    B. I and III
    C. II and III
    D. IV only

2. Which of the following transactions is exempt from the registration provisions of the USA?

    A. Isolated nonissuer transactions
    B. Unsolicited nonissuer transactions effected through a broker/dealer
    C. Transactions between issuers and underwriters
    D. All of the above

3. An agent would be acting illegally if she sold

    A. securities properly registered in a neighboring state but not registered in his home state
    B. federal covered securities not registered in the state
    C. revenue bonds of Illinois in Florida that were not registered in Florida
    D. securities guaranteed by a federal credit union organized under the laws of the state

4. Which of the following are exempt from state registration and advertising requirements?
    I. A nonissuer transaction in a security that has been outstanding for 2 months
    II. An isolated nonissuer transaction
    III. A transaction by an administrator of an estate
    IV. A transaction with no commissions directed by the offer or to more than 50 persons in the state who buy the security for investment purposes only

    A. I and II
    B. I and III
    C. II and III
    D. II and IV

5. All of the following transactions are exempt EXCEPT

    A. a transaction pursuant to an offer directed by the issuer to 20 nonaccredited persons in the state within a 12-month period where commissions are charged
    B. transactions by executors
    C. pledges of a security as collateral for a loan
    D. transactions in preorganization certificates if no commission is paid, no subscriber makes any payment, and the number of subscribers does not exceed 10

I. FRAUD

A. WILLFUL ATTEMPT TO DECEIVE FOR PROFIT OR GAIN *[make money or avoid losses]*

1. Fraud is any deliberate (knowing) concealment, lie, or half truth used to deceive someone for personal gain whether or not a transaction results

2. Under USA, "fraud is not limited to common law deceit"

B. NOT LIMITED TO JUDICIAL OR CASE-LAW DEFINITIONS BUT SUBJECT TO STATUTORY DEFINITIONS

C. FRAUD WHEN SELLING SECURITIES

1. Unlawful for any person in connection with offer, sale, or purchase of any security to

   a. Employ any device, scheme, or artifice to defraud

   b. Make untrue statement of material fact or omit a material fact

   c. Engage in any act, practice, or course of business that operates as a fraud or deceit upon any person with the intent to deceive

2. Penalties and sanctions for violation include

   a. Administrative proceedings (e.g., suspensions and revocations)—Administrator

   b. Judicial injunctions—courts

   c. Criminal and civil prosecutions—courts

II. PROHIBITED PRACTICES IN SALE OR OFFER OF SECURITIES

A. MISLEADING OR UNTRUE STATEMENTS

1. Inaccurate market quotations

No Borrowing From Mtg. Broker

    2. Incorrect statements of an issuer's earnings or projected earnings

    3. Inaccurate statements as to amount of commissions or markups/markdowns

    4. Telling customers that exchange listing is anticipated without knowledge of such

    5. Telling customers that a security registered with SEC or an Administrator has been approved by those regulators

B. FAILURE TO STATE IMPORTANT FACTS

    1. May not deliberately select or omit material information

    2. Agent is responsible for determining what is material

C. INSIDE INFORMATION

    1. May not make recommendations on basis of any inside information until it is made public

    2. May not repeat inside information except to report to supervisor or compliance officer

D. UNSUITABLE TRANSACTIONS

    1. Failure to make reasonable inquiry into customers' financial situations, needs, and investment objectives

    2. Recommending security transactions without reasonable grounds

E. CHURNING CUSTOMER ACCOUNTS

    1. Transactions excessive in size or frequency in view of customer resources or objectives

    2. Type of account—trading history

F. OTHER PROHIBITED BUSINESS PRACTICES RELATED TO BROKERAGE SERVICES

    1. Accepting orders on behalf of customers from a person other than the customer without prior written third-party trading authority

    2. Borrowing (lending) money or securities from customer unless in the business of lending money

    3. Commingling customer funds with agent's or firm's funds

    4. Deliberately failing to follow customer instructions

5. Effecting transactions without specific authority to do so

6. Effecting transactions not recorded on books of the agent's employer

7. Exercising discretionary authority without client's prior written authority

8. Failing to bring to attention of agent's employing broker/dealer customer written complaints

9. Failing to inform customers that certain transactions will involve larger than ordinary commissions

10. Guaranteeing customers a profit or guaranteeing against loss

11. Misrepresenting status of customer accounts

12. Making fictitious market quotations

13. Participating in transactions that create misleading appearance of active trading in a security: painting the Tape, wash sales, or matched purchases

14. Promising to perform services without intent or ability to perform

15. Sharing profits or losses with customers without customers' written consent and that of agent's employing broker/dealer; profits and losses must be in proportion to agent's personal funds invested

16. Soliciting orders for unregistered, nonexempt securities

17. Representing that registration with the state administrator conveys approval of an agent's or broker/dealer's qualifications

18. Sharing commissions on the sale of investment products with someone who is not an agent of the same or affiliated broker/dealer

19. Front running — *own/firm orders in front of customer*

Notebook Test 6

1. Deliberately failing to disclose sufficient information for a client to make an informed investment decision is
   A. a misuse of material inside information
   B. churning an account without discretion
   C. effecting transactions without specific authority
   D. a fraudulent business practice because a client must have sufficient information to make a rational decision

2. In which of the following situations did an agent commit fraud?
   A. A client claims an agent sold him securities that were unsuitable.
   B. Upon review of his files, an agent discovers he sold a nonexempt security that was unregistered.
   C. An agent sold an excellent growth company to a client by omitting immaterial information so as not to distract the client from purchasing a very suitable security.
   D. An agent knowingly sold a nonexempt, nonregistered security to a client who could not afford the risk involved.

3. Which of the following is commingling?
   A. Placing customer accounts in a common trust
   B. Placing mutual funds, cash, and securities in the same customer account
   C. Placing the broker/dealer's funds in the same account with nondiscretionary customers
   D. Borrowing money from a client and then putting those funds in the agent's personal account

4. A risk-averse investor wants to invest in Treasury securities, and the investor's agent recommends Treasury notes, pointing out that federal government-backed securities are riskless securities. In this situation, the agent has acted
   A. lawfully, because Treasury notes are suitable for a risk-averse customer and are free of all investment risk
   B. lawfully, because Treasury notes carry no risk of principal default
   C. unlawfully, because Treasury notes are unsuitable for a risk-averse customer
   D. unlawfully, because the agent failed to disclose that the investor carries interest rate risk but not default risk

5. An agent would be engaged in a prohibited practice if he
   I. shared commissions with other agents of his broker/dealer
   II. solicited a nonexempt, unregistered security to a nonaccredited investor
   III. shared both the gains and losses in a client's account with written approval in an amount proportionate to the amount invested in the account
   IV. aggressively traded on a daily basis a discretionary account with long-term growth as an objective
   A. I only
   B. II only
   C. II and IV
   D. I, II, III and IV

III. FRAUD WHEN PROVIDING INVESTMENT ADVISORY SERVICES

A. INVESTMENT ADVISORY ACTIVITIES

1. Investment advisers as fiduciaries are subject to additional ethical and disclosure standards, especially with respect to capacity in which they are acting and conflicts of interest

2. Unlawful for any person advising another person for compensation as to value of securities to

   a. Employ any device, scheme, or artifice to defraud the other person

   b. Engage in any act, practice, or course of business that operates as a fraud or deceit upon another person

   c. Act as principal for his own account knowingly to sell or purchase any security from a client, or knowingly act as agent for a person other than such client, without disclosing in writing the capacity in which acting and obtaining client's consent in writing

   d. Engage in dishonest or unethical practices as Administrator may define

B. COMMUNICATION WITH ADVISORY CLIENTS

C. INVESTMENT ADVISORY CONTRACTS

1. In writing

2. Services provided

3. Term

4. Fees

   a. May not be based on a percentage of increase in value or share of capital gains

   b. Exception: performance-based fees permitted in contract if client has net worth of $1.5 million or $750,000 under management

5. Formula for determining fees

*✱ wrap fees allowed
for IA say 1% of Net Asset Value*

6. Amount of prepaid fees to be refunded upon contract cancellation

7. Whether adviser has discretionary authority

8. Statement that contract may not be assigned without consent of client

9. If partnership, notify client of changes in partnership

    a) Death, withdrawal, or admission of partners with minority interest is not considered assignment

    b) Change in majority interest is considered assignment

D. CUSTODY OF FUNDS AND SECURITIES

1. Adviser may not take custody if Administrator prohibits custody, or in absence of rule, adviser fails to notify the Administrator.

2. Segregation of client securities; kept reasonably safe from destruction or loss

3. Client funds deposited to client only bank accounts

4. Immediate notification of change of location of funds/securities

5. Quarterly itemized statement to clients

6. Annual independent surprise audit to verify funds/securities

E. OTHER PROHIBITED PRACTICES RELATED TO ADVISORY ACTIVITIES

1. Misleading clients or prospective clients as to the qualifications for providing investment advice

2. Entering into an advisory contract without disclosing conflicts of interest, which could impair unbiased and objective advice

3. Failure to disclose commissions in addition to advisory fees

4. Disclosing identity, affairs, or investments of client to a third party without consent of client (unless required by law)

5. Discretion must be in writing, and contract cannot be assigned without customer written consent

6. Failure to disclose financial condition of adviser reasonably likely to impair adviser's ability to perform services

7. Failure to disclose legal or regulatory action against adviser material to evaluation of adviser's integrity or ability to meet contractual commitments

8. Failure to disclose within 48 hours before entering into an advisory contract that adviser was convicted within the last 10 years of securities-related violations by an Administrator, court, or self-regulatory agency (SRO)

9. Failure to disclose agency cross-transactions

   a. Transaction where the adviser acts as an agent for both the advisory client and another party on the contra (other) side of the trade

   b. The adviser must

   1.) Disclose the nature of the relationship

   2.) Obtain prior written consent of the client—indicate on confirmations that client may withdraw consent at any time

   3.) Accept only on an unsolicited basis—cannot recommend transaction to both sides of the transaction

10. Failure to provide wrap fee disclosures—nature of the program must be disclosed

   a. Charge a fixed fee for portfolio management, advice, and execution

   b. Must disclose that wrap fee may cost more than purchasing services separately

11. Use of third-party reports without acknowledging source—statistical reports not included

12. Use of any advertisements that

   a. Contain untrue statements

   b. Refer directly or indirectly to any testimonial

   c. Refer to past specific recommendations of the investment adviser unless all past performance is included and certain accounts are not selected to exaggerate performance

1. Which of the following activities is prohibited by the USA?

   I. A client insistently requests participation in an unsuitable investment, so the agent deliberately underreports the prospects of the investment to deter the client from making the purchase.
   II. An agent takes an order from the client's attorney without written trading authorization.
   III. An agent takes an order from the secretary of a nondiscretionary client who is too busy to give the order himself.
   IV. An agent encourages a client to act on a security on the basis of material inside information but is scrupulously careful not to disclose the source of the information to the client.

   A. I only
   B. I and II
   C. I, II and IV
   D. I, II, III and IV

2. Which of the following practices is fraudulent?

   A. Failing to state all the facts related to a security
   B. Selling a security to a customer with a commission that exceeds industry standards
   C. Marking up a security by 10% more than industry standards with the customer's knowledge and consent
   D. Marking up a security by 5%, but indicating to the client that the markup is only 2%

3. Which of the following is NOT a prohibited practice?

   I. The sale of high-grade, tax-exempt securities to a low-income client with long-term aggressive growth as his primary objective
   II. A certified financial planner indicates to customers that he is certified by the Administrator to conduct quantitative securities analysis
   III. An investment adviser representative identifies his clients to prospects by name and account balances, giving examples that accurately support his sales and performance claims
   IV. After several weeks spent establishing a client's trust, an adviser representative then discloses to the client that he was convicted of a nonsecurities-related misdemeanor in France

   A. I and II
   B. I and IV
   C. II and III
   D. IV only

4. It is unlawful for an investment adviser to

   I. share in the profits of an account in relation to the amount of time devoted to the account
   II. unilaterally transfer an account to another firm if the assets fall below a minimum level
   III. take custody of a client's securities and funds in the absence of a rule on custody by the state Administrator
   IV. fail to disclose to clients the departure of a general partner of an investment advisory partnership who only had a minority interest in the firm

   A. I only
   B. I and IV
   C. I, II and III
   D. I, II and IV

5. Which of the following statements regarding brokerage and advisory activities under the USA are TRUE?

    I. It is not unlawful for an adviser or broker to employ any device, scheme, or artifice to defraud in the sales of securities to institutional investors because the USA is designed to protect individual investors.

    II. Under the USA, it is unlawful for an investment adviser to deceive a person when not providing advice to that person.

    III. Sanctions for both advisers and brokers include administrative proceedings, judicial injunctions, and civil and criminal prosecutions.

    IV. It is unlawful for any person, whether technically defined as an investment adviser or not, to deceive another person for compensation as to the value of securities.

A. I and II
B. I and III
C. II and IV
D. III and IV

Unit 4
Administrative Provisions of the Uniform Securities Act

I. TERMS

A. SALE OR SELL—DISPOSITION OF A SECURITY FOR VALUE

1. Does not include stock dividend or stock split if stockholders give nothing of value

2. Does not include stock received as result of merger or consolidation

3. Pledge or loan, such as broker's loan of securities to customer, is not a sale

B. OFFER AND OFFER TO SELL

1. Attempt to dispose of a securities—offer to sell

2. Solicitation of any offer to buy

3. Assessable versus nonassessable stock

II. POWERS OF THE ADMINISTRATOR

A. MAKE RULES AND ORDERS

1. Issue interpretive releases

2. Rules/orders are not part of the USA—rules or orders of Administrator have the same authority as provisions of act

3. Persons may appeal an order in court within 60 days

B. CONDUCT INVESTIGATIONS AND ISSUE SUBPOENAS

1. Investigate within or outside of state

2. Administer oaths and affirmations; subpoena witnesses

3. Compel attendance, take evidence, and require production of documents

4. Make prohibitory orders and seek injunctions

5. Publish information concerning any violation

C. ISSUE CEASE AND DESIST ORDERS

1. In anticipation of violation

2. Without prior hearing

3. Hearing granted within 15 days if requested in writing

D. DENY, SUSPEND, OR REVOKE REGISTRATION

1. Administrator may deny, revoke, or suspend any registration, or bar or restrict activities of the registrant if it is in the public interest and the registrant does any of the following

   a. Files false or incomplete application

   b. Willfully violates any provision of the act

   c. Was convicted of misdemeanor involving securities or any felony within last 10 years

   d. Has been enjoined by any court or SRO from engaging in securities business

   e. Is the subject of an order of any Administrator denying, suspending, or revoking registration

   f. Is insolvent

      1.) In case of a broker/dealer or investment adviser, a formal finding of insolvency is required

      2.) In case of agents or IARs, only if a control person

   g. Willfully violates foreign banking or securities law

   h. Is not qualified on the basis of training and knowledge

2. However, the Administrator

   a. May not deny registration solely on basis of lack of experience, if applicant is qualified by training, knowledge, or both

   b. May take into consideration supervision of a broker/dealer or investment adviser

   c. May consider an adviser not necessarily qualified solely on the basis of experience as a broker/dealer or agent

   3. Administrator may require written or oral examination

   4. Administrator may summarily suspend pending registration—applicant has 15 days to request a hearing

E. NO ORDER OTHER THAN SUMMARY POSTPONEMENT MAY BE ENTERED WITHOUT

   1. Prior notice

   2. Opportunity for hearing

   3. Written findings of fact and conclusions of law

F. NONPUNITIVE TERMINATION—REGISTRATION CANCELLATION

   1. Withdrawal effective 30 days after filing if no revocations or suspensions are pending

   2. Administrator may institute an action for a revocation or suspension within 1 year after withdrawal has become effective

   3. Cancellation of registration is not punitive

   a. Deceased

   b. Cannot be found

   c. Ceased to do business

   d. Declared mentally incompetent

III. PENALTIES FOR VIOLATING THE USA

A. CRIMINAL PENALTIES

   1. Fines up to $5,000, imprisonment for up to 3 years, or both

   2. Statute of limitations/no indictment after 5 years from alleged violation

   3. No person may be imprisoned if he proves no knowledge of rule or order

B. CIVIL LIABILITIES

   1. Statute of limitations—sooner of

   a. Three years from date of alleged violation or

      b. Two years from date of discovery of violation

  2. Recovery of amount paid for security or advice with interest less amount received from security plus reasonable legal and court costs.

  3. Rescission

      a. Seller of security or advice may offer to repurchase security for amount paid plus interest

      b. Buyer may not sue if received written offer from seller and failed to reject offer within 30 days

IV. JUDICIAL REVIEW OF ORDERS

A. REVIEW (APPEAL)

Person affected by Administrator's order may obtain review (appeal) by filing position in appropriate court within 60 days

V. SCOPE OF THE ACT

A. APPLIES TO PERSONS WHO SELL OR OFFER TO SELL IF

  1. Originated in Administrator's state

  2. Directed to Administrator's state

  3. Accepted in Administrator's state

B. BROADCAST AND PUBLISHING EXCEPTION TO JURISDICTION

  1. Offer not considered made in state if received through television, radio broadcast, Internet, or newspapers outside state

  2. Bona fide newspaper or periodical published inside state but has 66.7% circulation outside state

C. ADMINISTRATOR MAY COOPERATE WITH OTHER AGENCIES

1. Other states

2. NASD, SEC, and so forth

1. In conducting investigations, the Administrator does not have the power to

   A. publish information about an investment adviser's violation of the USA

   B. apply to a state court to compel a witness to comply with a subpoena

   C. make cease and desist orders without a prior hearing

   D. sentence violators to imprisonment within prescribed limits

2. All of the following are unethical or prohibited practices EXCEPT

   A. failing to disclose commissions in addition to advisory fees

   B. divulging names and financial data on clients in response to a subpoena

   C. misrepresenting the status of a client's account

   D. failing to disclose the precarious financial condition that could impair an adviser's ability to perform services

3. A registration can be denied or revoked if it is in the public interest and a registrant

   I. fails to disclose the fact that he was convicted of a nonsecurities-related misdemeanor within the last 2 years

   II. has willfully violated the securities laws of a foreign jurisdiction

   III. is qualified on the basis of knowledge and training but lacks requisite experience

   IV. has engaged in dishonest or unethical practices in the securities business

   A. I and II

   B. I and III

   C. II and IV

   D. III and IV

4. Which of the following statements are TRUE?

   I. An Administrator can suspend a pending registration on a summary basis.

   II. An Administrator may not summarily issue a stop order without prior notice and opportunity for a hearing.

   III. An Administrator may cancel a registration for the same reasons the Administrator revoked or suspended a registration.

   A. I and II

   B. I and III

   C. II and III

   D. I, II and III

5. Which of the following statements describe the powers of the Administrator over the issuance of orders?

   I. A final order may be appealed in the appropriate court within 60 days of the order being issued.

   II. Appeal of a final order will act as a stay of the order unless a court of competent jurisdiction rules to the contrary.

   III. No final order may be issued without the opportunity for a hearing.

   IV. Final orders must receive approval from the state legislature.

   A. I and II

   B. I and III

   C. I and IV

   D. II and IV

1. **B.** A person is generally anybody who can open an account. A minor cannot open an account or enter into contracts and so is not considered a legal person.

2. **C.** The USA authorizes the governor or legislature of a state to designate an agency, or person, as Administrator (or Commissioner) to administer the act in the state. The Securities and Exchange Commission is the federal agency, not state agency, that oversees and regulates securities on a national level.

3. **D.** An unincorporated investment club, an individual who buys and sells securities for his own account, associations, and partnerships (whether or not they issue certificates), and the US government are specifically listed as persons in the act. Minor children, deceased individuals, and mentally incompetent individuals are not persons under the act.

4. **B.** An agent represents a broker/dealer in conducting securities sales or transactions. A broker/dealer is not an agent; agents usually work for broker/dealers. Agents are excluded from the definition of agent if they have no place of business in the state and sell securities to an existing client who is not a resident of the state.

5. **A.** A broker/dealer by definition is not an agent. An individual who sells US government securities in exempt transactions is not an agent provided there is no compensation linked to the sale. An individual who represents an issuer in a nonexempt transaction is an agent. Under virtually all circumstances, an individual receiving compensation related to securities sales is defined as an agent.

1. **D.** Clerical and ministerial personnel, full time or temporary, are not included in the definition of investment adviser representatives (supervised persons) or in the definition of investment advisers. Other persons associated with an investment adviser, including officers of the firm, are generally considered to be investment adviser representatives. An investment adviser representative is not an investment adviser in the same manner that an agent is not a broker/dealer. A federal covered adviser is not, for definitional purposes, considered an adviser under the USA to avoid duplicate regulation by both the state and the federal government.

2. **C.** A person with an office in the state who sells securities to residents or nonresidents of the state is a broker/dealer as defined in the USA. A person with no office in the state who sells exempt or nonexempt securities to financial institutions is not defined as a broker/dealer under the USA.

3. **D.** An adviser with no place of business in the state who conducts business with insurance companies is exempt from registration in the state. If an agent is hired away from a broker/dealer by another broker/dealer, both broker/dealers and the agent must inform the Administrator. If an investment representative is hired away from a federal covered adviser by another federal covered adviser, only the investment adviser representative must inform the Administrator. If choice B had referred to a state covered investment adviser, then the correct statement would be that both advisers, but not the adviser representative, would make the notification.

4. **D.** An investment adviser need not register in a state if it has no place of business in the state and advises such institutional clients as investment companies; the number of clients is irrelevant. Generally, an investment adviser must register in a state if it has a place of business in the state. The de minimis exception from state registration applies only to investment advisors who have an office in the state and advise 5 or fewer public noninstitutional clients.

5. **C.** A federal covered adviser is an adviser with a federally imposed exemption from state registration. Securities issued by investment companies registered under the Investment Company Act of 1940 are included in the definition of federal covered security. Remember, federal covered securities are registered with the SEC, not with the states.

Notebook Test 3
Answers and Rationales

1. **A.** Fixed annuities are not securities; variable annuities are. Corporate equity is another way of saying stock and corporate debt is bonds and debentures.

2. **C.** The registration statement does have to include a listing of all states in which the offering will be registered, but only lists the amount being offered in this state.

3. **B.** The total amount of the security to be offered in other states need not be specified, although naming those states is required. The amount of the security to be offered in the state of registration is required because it generally provides the basis on which the registration fee is calculated. A stop order from another state that affects the offering of the security within the state must be included. The registration statement will always describe the intended use of the proceeds.

4. **B.** A corporation that proposes to issue securities and has not is still considered an issuer; merely proposing an issue is enough under the USA. Choices III and IV are also issuers because they are corporations that are in the act of issuing securities to the public. Broker/dealers trading for others are not acting in the capacity of issuers.

5. **C.** Any security may be registered by qualification, but it is required only if another method of registration is unavailable. The company in choice I must be SEC registered because its previous offering was in several states. Generally, an SEC-registered security that has been outstanding at least 90 days is exempt. Because the company in choice II will not have a federal registration statement, registration by coordination will not be available. The company in choice III will require federal registration in connection with the same offering, so registration by coordination will be available.

1. **D.** A federal covered security is a security that has a federally imposed exemption from registration. The security is then covered by federal legislation and, therefore, the states do not have regulatory jurisdiction over the security. A security the USA regulates is by definition not covered by federal registration requirements and therefore is not a covered security as used in the USA. Securities covered by the Investment Company Act of 1940, the US Federal Reserve (commercial bank securities), and securities issued by the US government are all covered by federal legislation and are covered securities.

2. **D.** Corporate stock sold publicly in the state is not exempt from registration. Bank stocks, public utility securities, and foreign government debt of countries with which the US has diplomatic relations are exempt securities.

3. **D.** The National Securities Markets Improvement Act preempts state registration of covered securities. NSMIA eliminated dual registration of securities and reduced the powers of state securities Administrators over securities registration. NSMIA does not require registration of securities sold intrastate.

4. **D.** An investment contract issued in connection with an employee pension plan, and securities issued by St. Paul's Catholic Church in Tempe, Arizona, by a public utility, or by the Canadian government are exempt from registration under the USA.

5. **B.** Any security listed on the NYSE, regardless of state of domicile of the corporation or the customer, is a federal covered security. Municipal bonds, exempt securities under the Securities Act of 1933, are also federal covered securities with one significant exception: if the issuer is a political entity in this state and it is sold to a resident of this state, it is not considered a federal covered security in this state.

1. **D.** A certified financial planner selling unlisted securities to numerous individual clients, regardless of their net worth, is engaged in a nonexempt transaction. This would not be true if the financial planner's clients were all financial institutions rather than individuals. Transactions by an administrator and an executor are exempt transactions, as are unsolicited nonissuer transactions. A pledge of stock as collateral for a loan is also an exempt transaction.

2. **D.** All of the transactions are exempt. Isolated nonissuer transactions, unsolicited transactions effected through a broker/dealer, and transactions between issuers and underwriters are exempt transactions under the provisions of the USA.

3. **A.** An agent cannot sell securities in a state unless she is registered or exempt from state registration. Federal covered, tax-exempt municipal bonds, and securities guaranteed by a federal credit union organized in the state are all exempt from registration.

4. **C.** Isolated nonissuer transactions and transactions by an Administrator are included in the list of exempt transactions; the others are nonexempt transactions. Nonissuer transactions must be outstanding 90 days to be exempt.

5. **A.** A transaction pursuant to an offer directed by the issuer to 20 persons in the state would not qualify as a private placement and therefore would not be exempt.

Notebook Test 6
Answers and Rationales

1. **D.** Failure to disclose sufficient information for a client to make an informed decision is a fraudulent practice. The other choices are prohibited practices, but not necessarily fraudulent.

2. **D.** Fraud requires the intent to deceive. The agent knowingly deceived the client by offering an unsuitable investment.

3. **C.** Commingling is mixing client funds or securities with those of the broker/dealer, whether discretionary or not. Placing funds in a common trust is not commingling and is not prohibited. Accounts with several types of securities in them is not commingling. Borrowing money from a client is prohibited, but is not commingling.

4. **D.** Although Treasury securities (such as T-notes issued by the federal government) do not carry default risk, the customer who buys them bears interest rate risk because the value of the notes will fall if interest rates rise. The agent has acted unlawfully in not disclosing this to the customer.

5. **C.** An agent cannot lawfully solicit an unregistered, nonexempt security to a nonaccredited investor. Day trading in an account with long-term growth as an objective would constitute an unsuitable transaction and, therefore, is prohibited under USA. Sharing commissions is only permitted with agents of the same or affiliated broker/dealers.

1. **D.** An agent cannot take trading orders from anyone but the client unless he has written authorization on file. An agent cannot act on the basis of material inside information whether he keeps it confidential or not. While choice I may, in fact, be in the client's best interest, deliberate misrepresentation is prohibited.

2. **D.** Marking up a security by more than industry practices is a prohibited practice but is not necessarily fraudulent. Choice D is fraudulent even though the commission or markup was modest because the agent knowingly deceived the client by lying.

3. **D.** An agent or investment adviser representative need not disclose nonsecurities-related misdemeanors. The other activities are all prohibited. Selling tax-exempt bonds to a low-income client is prohibited because it is unsuitable. A certified financial planner cannot lawfully indicate that he is certified by the Administrator to conduct quantitative analysis. If registered in a state, the planner can only indicate that he is registered in the state. Investment advisers must keep their clients and their transactions confidential unless under a legal order to provide disclosure or prior permission has been obtained from the client.

4. **D.** An investment adviser cannot share in the profits of an account on the basis of time devoted and may not assign an account without the written permission of the client. An investment adviser must disclose to clients when any partner, minority interest or not, departs from the firm.

5. **D.** Sanctions for violations are administrative proceedings, judicial injunctions, and civil and criminal prosecutions. No individual, whether technically defined as an adviser or not, may deceive another person when providing investment advice if he is compensated for providing the advice. As long as there is no advisory client relationship, people can deceive each other and it does not violate the USA.

Notebook Test 8
Answers and Rationales

1. **D.** The Administrator does not have the legal authority to sentence a violator to prison; only a court with proper jurisdiction can do that. The Administrator does have the authority to apply to a court to sentence a violator and can publish information concerning violations.

2. **B.** Investment professionals must divulge confidential client information under subpoena. All the other practices are unethical. Choice D relates specifically to those advisers that maintain custody of customer's funds or securities or receive prepayments of fees in the amount of more than $500 for 6 or more months of advisory service.

3. **C.** An Administrator may not deny a registration solely on the basis of lack of experience. An Administrator may deny, revoke, or suspend a registration if it is in the public interest and a registrant fails to disclose the fact that he has been convicted of a securities-related misdemeanor (or any felony) within the last 10 years. The Administrator may also deny a registration if a registrant has engaged in dishonest or unethical practices and it is in the public interest to deny the registration. Registration can also be denied if a registrant violated securities laws of a foreign country.

4. **B.** An Administrator can, on a summary basis, suspend a pending registration but may not issue a stop order without a prior notice and an opportunity for a hearing. Cancellation is different from revocation. Cancellation is not a result of disciplinary action and occurs when the registrant no longer exists, ceases to do business, is declared mentally incompetent, or cannot be located.

5. **B.** Any final order of the Administrator may be appealed as long as it is done within 60 days of the order. The appeal does not act as a stay of the order. Only a court of competent jurisdiction may issue a stay of the order. Because the final order is similar to passing sentence, an opportunity for a hearing must be granted. The Administrator's orders have nothing to do with the state legislature.

A, B, C . . . Pass the 63!

KAPLAN FINANCIAL'S ANSWERPHONE PRESENTS A FUN WAY TO STUDY

Administrator: The state Administrator is responsible for the administration of the Uniform Securities Act. An Administrator has vast powers but cannot issue a permanent order of denial, suspension, or revocation against any person or security without first informing them of the opportunity to request a hearing. Requests for hearings must be made within 15 days. The role of the Administrator is highly testable.

Broker/Dealers: A broker/dealer is not by definition an agent, issuer, or bank. When you complete your exams (and register), you will be an agent of your firm. Most likely, your firm is a broker/dealer.

Coordination: Registration of nonexempt securities in a state can be accomplished by two methods: coordination and qualification. Expect a question on each method. Coordination would most likely be used for a large IPO. A small corporation selling its first public shares on an intrastate basis would probably use qualification (the more stringent method).

Deliberately: When you deliberately omit a material fact, you are committing fraud. When you deliberately do not follow a customer's instructions, you are engaging in a prohibited business practice. On the exam, certain words are tip-offs to what a question is about. When you see the word *deliberately*, something prohibited will likely follow.

Exemptions: Exemptions always drive test takers crazy. Here are some handy tips: exemptions make perfectly good sense. Nobody wants to register. Being nonexempt means that you must comply and adhere to the Uniform Securities Act. In other words, securities that are nonexempt have to register. It is costly and time consuming to register. Banks and insurance companies are exempt because they have their own rules and regulations. Identify whether it is a security or a transaction that is exempt. With the exception of unsolicited trades and isolated nonissuer transactions, exempt transactions generally do not involve the public. For instance, a transaction between an issuer and an underwriter is an exempt transaction. It is unlawful for broker/dealers or agents to solicit nonexempt unregistered securities. There is no rule against soliciting exempt securities. For instance, there is no problem if an agent calls a customer and sells some US Treasury bonds (exempt). No securities are exempt from the antifraud provisions of the Uniform Securities Act.

Federal covered advisers: Investment advisers who manage $30 million or more register at the federal level (SEC). The term *federal covered adviser* may appear on the exam, but the test is primarily concerned with investment advisers relating to the Uniform Securities Act.

Guarantee: The word *guarantee* should be used very sparingly in the securities industry. It is improper to guarantee an investment as being profitable.

Hours: We recommend at least 30–40 hours of preparation for the Series 63. Use your study time wisely by practicing questions.

Investment advisers: The exam is notorious for difficult questions about investment advisers. An investment adviser representative is not an investment adviser. Also, a broker/dealer or agent who receives no compensation for investment advice is excluded from the definition of investment adviser. Many stockbrokers give investment advice all day long, but they are not investment advisers. Successful completion of the Series 65 or 66 is necessary to be an investment adviser representative.

Jail: Violations of the Uniform Securities Act can result in a maximum penalty of 3 years in prison or a $5,000 fine for each violation or both.

Know the easy stuff. The test allows you to miss 18 of 60 questions. There are approximately 25 relatively easy questions. Don't miss any of these. If you get the 25 easy questions correct, you can miss 17 of the 35 hard questions. We like those odds.

Lawyers: Lawyers, accountants, teachers, and engineers whose advice is incidental to their professions specifically are excluded from the definition of investment adviser. A geologist, for instance, is not specifically excluded. Beware of this topic!

Market manipulation: This is a strictly prohibited activity with the intent of causing security prices to move unrelated to supply and demand. Examples include front-running, painting the Tape, and matched orders.

Not a security: Ordinary insurance policies, endowments, fixed annuities, Keogh plans, IRAs, commodity contracts, and precious metals are not considered securities under the Uniform Securities Act. A commodity options contract is a security.

Offer: An offer is an attempt to dispose of a security for value, or the solicitation of an offer to buy a security. If an agent of a broker/dealer makes an offer in a state, then he must be registered in that state.

Persons: Corporations, partnerships, individuals, and political subdivisions are all considered persons under the act. Memory jogger: anyone who can open an account is considered a person.

Qualifications: The Administrator cannot deny a registration solely on the basis of lack of experience.

Registration: All securities professionals' registrations expire on December 31 unless renewed by the Administrator. This is a highly testable point.

Sale: A sale is a contract to sell or the disposition of a security for value. A gift of assessable stock is a sale.

Two years: A civil suit may not be brought in a state more than 2 years after discovery or 3 years from the date of sale, whichever comes first. The statute of limitations for a criminal violation is 5 years after the alleged violation. A conviction of any felony in the past 10 years is a statutory bar from registration. The exam has very few questions that will have a number as an answer. This works against your chances. Memorization questions are too easy.

U-4 and U-5 forms: There may be a question on each. Both the agent and broker/dealer are required to notify the Administrator when the agent terminates his employment (U-5).

Voting trust certificates: Voting trust certificates are considered securities under the act. This could be on the exam.

Whiskey warehouse receipts: Whiskey warehouse receipts are considered securities under the act. This could be on the exam.

Xylophone: Xylophone players need to score 70% to pass this exam . . . so do you.

You: You are an agent when you file your consent to service of process, pass an examination, post a surety bond, (if necessary), and have been notified by your supervisor that you are registered. Investment advisers and broker/dealers must meet the same criteria, but they must also meet a minimum net capital requirement.

Z-tranches: Not on the exam. Phew!

This is intended to be used as an amusing supplement to your study materials. It is NOT comprehensive. Please call AnswerPhone at **1-800-621-9621**, ext. 3598 if you have questions.